The Origins of Wisdom

MYSTICISM

O. B. DUANE

First published in Great Britain in 1997 by
Brockhampton Press,
20 Bloomsbury Street,
London WC1B 3QA
A member of the Hodder Headline Group.

ISBN 1 86019 552 0

A copy of the C.I.P. data is available from
the British Library upon request.

Produced for Brockhampton Press by Flame Tree Publishing,
a part of The Foundry Creative Media Company Limited,
The Long House, Antrobus Road, Chiswick, London W4 5HY

The Origins of Wisdom

MYSTICISM

O. B. DUANE

BROCKHAMPTON PRESS

Foreword

❋

I can recall so clearly when I first became aware of a greater and deeper potential in Christianity than I had been led to expect. It was a grey winter's after-
noon and I had walked in meditation of nature, some fifteen miles over the
hills to the ancient cathedral of Wells. Entering, I stumbled upon Sung
Evensong and found myself caught up 'even to heaven' by I knew not what
forces. I felt at one with all around me and the choir's singing seemed as the
voices of all creation joining in praise.

It scared the life out of me! No one had prepared me for this. How I wish
I had had this book then. For through the chronicling of the history and development of Christian mysticism, it becomes clear that such experiences and the
quest to both understand and be part of them, is as old, indeed older, than
Christianity. I hope this book, packed with quotes which offer windows to the
soul and to God, will inspire many to reach out and affirm their own potential
for mysticism.

Martin Palmer, Director of ICOREC
January 1997

*Mystics believe that Purification is the only process by
which obstacles to a union with God may be removed.*

Contents

✻

To achieve communion with the Divine is the goal of all Mysticism.

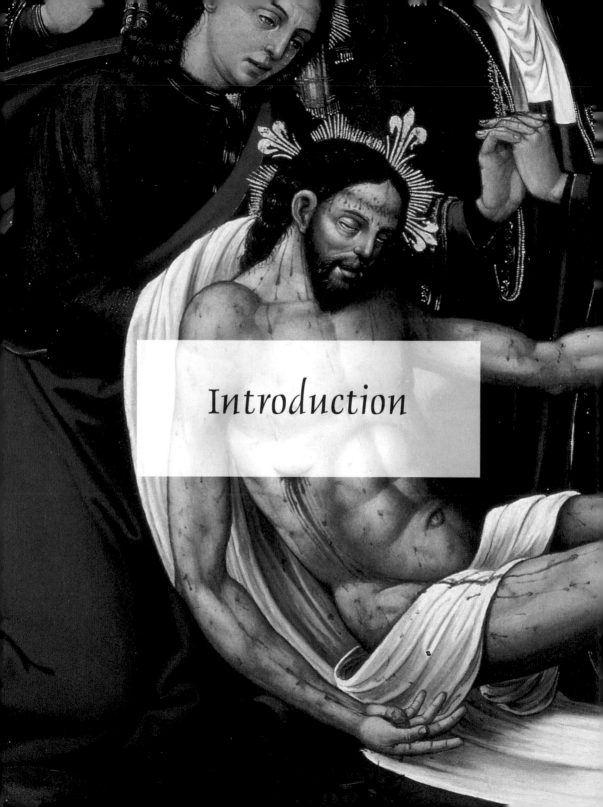

Introduction

Introduction

❋

> The kingdom of God is within us, even in this life; for this life's reward is holiness, the vision of God; its punishment, that of being what sinners are. This vision or knowledge of the Most High is the direct personal communion of a soul that no longer reasons, but feels and knows.
>
> *Philo* (c. 13 BC—AD 45)

'MYSTICISM' IS A VERY BROAD TERM which has been used over the centuries to describe many different things, from Christian science to spiritualism, to revelations and visions, to occultism and magic. The original word is derived from the ancient Greek root meaning 'to close' or 'to shut' and was first used by the Greeks in connection with the Eleusinian mysteries, to describe those individuals who had gained an esoteric knowledge of Divine things and who were expected to keep this sacred knowledge strictly to themselves.

Philosophers during the centuries immediately preceding the birth of Christ, among them Socrates and Plato, appropriated the word 'mysticism' and applied it to their own speculative doctrines on the spiritual nature of man. Later,

The study of Mysticism strives to liberate the human soul, to find peace in a union with God.

when the Christian Church began to emerge under the influence of the quietism and introspection of later Neo-Platonism, the derivation of the word was enlarged to include in its meaning the closing of the mind to influences of the external world and the development of a higher consciousness of the self.

The subject of this book is Christian Mysticism, for it is not within the scope of this volume to discuss the Mystics of India and the East. Mysticism, however, cannot be confined to a single religion, and must be viewed as 'the raw material of all religions'. To achieve communion with the Divine, the Ultimate Reality, is the endeavour of all Mysticism, and this is equally true of Christianity, Buddhism, Sufism, or the Mysticism of Islam. As the scholar Margaret Smith puts it: 'While religion in general separates the Divine from the human, Mysticism, going beyond religion, aspires to intimate union with the Divine, to a penetration of the Divine within the soul and to a disappearance of the individuality, with all its modes of acting, thinking and feeling, in the Divine substance.'[1]

Eastern Mystics differ from Christian Mystics in their conception of the Divine. The Buddhist, for example, sets out to attain perfect Enlightenment, a state of being which he understands as the Ultimate Reality, and he does not seek a relationship with a personal God. The goal of Christian Mysticism, on the other hand, is to forge a profoundly personal relationship with the Creator, to experience, through contemplation, the very Presence of an individual God. Indeed, in a Christian context, it would be more accurate to substitute the word 'Mysticism' for 'Contemplation', since the word 'mystical' was not widely used until the later Middle Ages. 'Contemplation' is the word used by St Augustine, St Gregory and St Bernard to describe what is now commonly referred to as 'the mystical experience.'

How does the Christian then achieve this 'intimate union' with the Divine? How does he arrive at a unity of the self with God? The philosopher Plotinus,

Ancient philosophers adopted the term 'mysticism' and applied it to their theories on the spiritual nature of man.

(c. 203-262 AD), although himself a non-Christian, declared that God was 'external to no man', but qualified this statement by adding that 'even if the eye could not behold the sun unless it were itself sunlike, so neither could the soul behold God if it were not Godlike.' [2]

There is hardly any soil, be it ever so barren, where Mysticism will not strike root; hardly any creed, however formal, round which it will not twine itself. It is, indeed, the eternal cry of the human soul for rest; the insatiable longing of a being wherein infinite ideals are fettered and cramped by a miserable actuality; and so long as man is less than an angel and more than a beast, this cry will not for a moment fail to make itself heard.

E G Browne (1862—1926), A Year Among the Persians

Speculative Mysticism enabled the individual to become aware of what he was seeking and allowed for the possibility that the human soul could be united with the Creator,[3] but this went hand in hand with a practical system, and certain fundamental doctrines needed to be observed before the individual could expect to attain his goal.

Opposite: Mystics sought to achieve a personal relationship with God, through mystical experience, or contemplation.
Overleaf: On the path to attaining a union with the Creator, the Mystic must be guided by Love.

The four basic assumptions of Mysticism, or 'articles of faith', as W. R. Inge refers to them, are as follows:

Firstly, Mysticism supports the belief that the soul is as real as any other organ of the body and in its proper sphere controls our spiritual welfare, allowing us to discern spiritual truth.

Secondly, we must all be partakers of the Divine nature. In other words, we cannot possibly have true knowledge of God unless we acknowledge that we all have within us a Divine 'spark', a tiny glint of Divine light which seeks to be re-united with the Eternal Flame.

Thirdly, Mysticism postulates that Purification is the only process by which we may remove the obstacles to our union with God. Loss of selfhood is the only route to a proper relationship with the Absolute Being.

Fourthly, our guide on the upward path must be Love. To the mystic, regardless of whatever type of religion he adheres to, 'the Object of his search is conceived of as the Beloved, and the mystic regards himself as the lover, yearning for the consummation of his love in union with the One he loves.'[4]

> ## This union is within us of our naked nature and were this nature to be separated from God it would fall into nothingness.
>
> *John Ruysbroeck (1293—1381)*

As Christ took the path to Calvary, so the Mystics sought their own Ways to salvation.

> The Beloved drew near to the Lover, to comfort and console him for the grief which he suffered and the tears which he shed. And the nearer was the Lover to the Beloved, the more he grieved and wept, crying out upon the dishonour which his Beloved endured.
>
> Book of the Lover and the Beloved, (Verse 124)

The Mystic Way

The Way which must be followed by those seeking to attain Mystic freedom is clearly set out in the Theologia Germanica, an anonymous book of devotion thought to have been written in Germany some time towards the end of the thirteenth century. Its teachings, which were derived from those of the ancient Greek scholars, were generally accepted by Christian Mystics as a practical guide to achieving communion with the Beloved. According to the book the steps of the upward path are divided into three stages, the Way of Purgation, the Way of Illumination and the Way of Union.

Pilgrims entered into a contemplative life in order to purify their souls and attain Mystic freedom.

The Way of Purgation (Purgative Life)

By repentance, confession and amendment, the self will be cleansed and selfhood annihilated. Plotinus insisted that this should not necessarily dictate a life of asceticism, and Philo later supported this argument, insisting that no one should enter into the contemplative life before the age of fifty after having first exercised faithfully the duties and functions of family and civic life. Yet for many Mystics, particularly those of the East, and those of the early Christian Church, withdrawal from the world has been judged the only way that the soul may be purified of its sins.

The Way of Illumination (Illuminative Life)

Once the external life has come under scrutiny and been amended in accordance with the Eternal Will, the struggle of the inner life begins. All the faculties – feeling, intellect and will – must be concentrated upon God. This stage is described by E. Underhill as 'the complete surrender of man's personal striving to the overruling Will of God and thus the linking up of all the successive acts of life with the Abiding.' [5]

The Way of Union (Unitive Life)

The final stage of the Way is the Unitive or Contemplative life, the highest of all possible conditions, in which the pilgrim confronts God face to face and is at one with Him. This experience is accompanied by feelings of ecstasy and joy and frequently by revelations or visions, as all consciousness of self evaporates and the soul becomes transformed in God. Mystics such as Louis of Blois, a Benedictine Abbot living in the sixteenth century, described the Unitive experience as follows:

At the final stage, the Unitive Life, the pilgrim confronts God in a pure and divine union.

It is a great thing, an exceeding great thing, in the time of this exile to be joined to God in the divine light by a mystical and denuded union. This takes place where a pure, humble, and resigned soul, burning with ardent love, is carried above itself by the grace of God and, through the brilliancy of the divine light shining on the mind, it loses all consideration and distinction of things, and lays aside all, and, as it were, reduced to nothing, it melts away into God.

[1]   Margaret Smith, *History of Mysticism* London 1930, pp. 3-4
[2]   Plotinus, *The Enneads*, trans. S. McKenna, London 1956
[3]   Christianity and Theism has many words for God, including 'The Absolute', 'Absolute Being', 'Absolute Reality' as well as 'The Creator'.
[4]   Margaret Smith, *History of Mysticism* London 1930, p. 6
[5]   E. Underhill, *Man and the Supernatural*, p. 246

The Way of Union is accompanied by feelings of ecstasy and often by revelations.

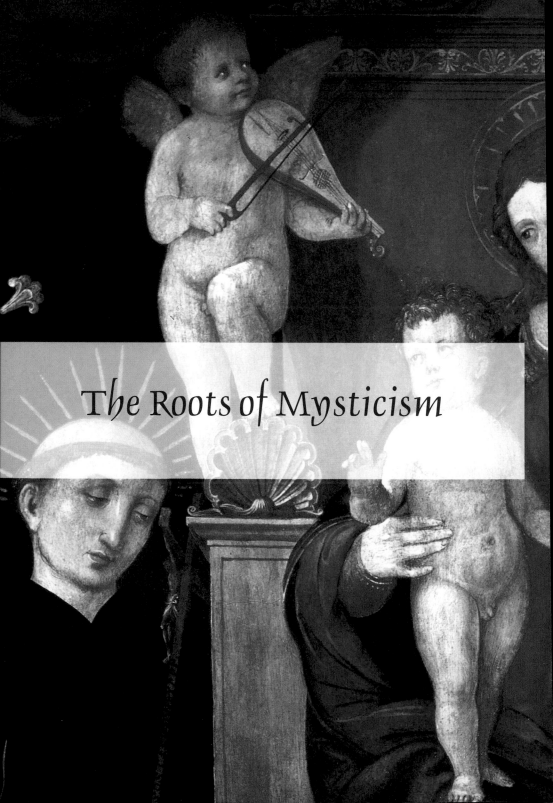

The Roots of Mysticism

The Roots of Mysticism

❈

THE ATTEMPT TO DISCOVER the earliest roots of Christian Mysticism takes us far back through time to the classical period of ancient Greece. Although this pre-dates Christianity, it accommodated the vigorous development of intellectual and artistic life that exercised so powerful an influence on the evolution of institutionalized religions such as Judaism, Christianity and Islam, and the whole concept of 'mystical experience.'

Mysticism and the Ancient Greeks

Bearing in mind that the word 'Mysticism' actually comes from ancient Greece, it is hardly surprising to find a mystical element in nearly all Greek philosophy. The philosopher Socrates (469-399 BC) was perhaps one of the first exponents of speculative mysticism, whose inclination towards a belief in the immortality of the soul and its kinship with the Divine was passed on to, and further developed by, his pupil Plato (c. 428-348 BC). Generally accepted as the father of European Mysticism, Plato asserts that the soul once shared a previous existence with the true Being and therefore continues to manifest an instinctive longing to be at one with this Being once again. 'But all souls do not easily recall the things of the other world,' he asserts in the Phraedus; 'they may have seen them for a short time only ... or they may have had their hearts turned to unrighteousness through some corrupting influence', allowing them to lose the memory of what they once saw.

The philosopher Socrates was one of the first exponents of speculative mysticism.

The soul recognizes this world as a reflection only of the truly Real and has in itself an 'eye' for divine Reality. The ascent to the truly Real can only be made by the soul, which must first release itself as far as it can from all intercourse or contact with the body. The guide leading the soul is Love. From love of one beautiful form springs a love of all, and an understanding of the true Beauty:

> Do you not see that in that region alone where he sees beauty with the faculty capable of seeing it, will he be able to bring forth not mere reflected images of goodness but true goodness, because he will be in contact not with a reflection but with the truth? And having brought forth and nurtured true goodness he will have the privilege of being beloved of God, and becoming, if ever a man can, immortal himself.
>
> Plato (428–348 BC), Symposium

Mysticism and the Bible

The Old Testament Book of Genesis informs us that 'God created man in the image of himself, in the image of God he created him, male and female he created them.' (Genesis: 27) The relationship between God and man in Paradise before the Fall was one of intimate union. Adam's disobedience led to the degradation of

Mystics strive to achieve for themselves the union between God and Adam before the Fall.

man, and Christians understand the Scriptures which follow this account to be a call to the full restoration of man's image and likeness in Christ. The journeys of Abraham, Jacob, Moses, the prophets and Psalmists towards personal communion with God can all be interpreted as mystical experiences to some degree. The prophet Isaiah, and the prophet Jeremiah, for example, employ the mystic image of the lover and the Beloved when discussing the relation of God and the soul. Jeremiah 2: 2 states: 'Yahweh says this: "I remember your faithful love, the affection of your bridal days, when you followed me through the desert, through a land unsown."' Later, in his 'Confessions', Jeremiah compares himself to one who has been 'seduced' and 'overpowered' by his God (20: 7). Isaiah, using a similar image (61:10) treats his relationship with God as a form of marital union: 'For he has clothed me in garments of salvation, he has wrapped me in a cloak of saving justice, like a bridegroom wearing his garland, like a bride adorned in her jewels. '

As with the philosophers of ancient Greece, the Psalmist recognized that the Divine 'spark' lay within: 'Where shall I go to escape your spirit? Where shall I flee from your presence? If I scale the heavens you are there, if I lie flat in Sheol, there you are.' (139:7) The Psalmist was very keen to foster the Divine Presence and yearned for the repose of final fulfilment within, frequently describing the laws by which he hoped to achieve this: 'Whoever lives blamelessly, who acts uprightly, who speaks the truth from the heart, who keeps the tongue under control ... ' (Psalm 15: 2). Psalm 46 is one which points most clearly, however, to a mystic interpretation of knowledge of God, since it foreshadows the Unitive Way of all later Mystics: 'Be still and acknowledge that I am God'. During the final stage of contemplation, all thought and reasoning are abandoned, all preoccupation with the self set aside, and God is intimately absorbed in this silent domain.

Opposite: Many Psalms point to a mystic interpretation of the knowledge of God; an understanding that the Divine spark lay within.
Overleaf: St John's Gospel is considered the ideal of Christian Mysticism and is influenced by the writings of the early philosophers.

Omine ne in furore tuo ar
guas me: neq; in ira tua cor
ripias me,
Miserere mei domine qm

The New Testament

Two individuals, John the Evangelist and St Paul, introduced a more fully developed Mysticism into the New Testament. 'The Gospel of St John', according to W. R. Inge, 'is the charter of Christian Mysticism. Indeed, Christian Mysticism ... might almost be called Johannine Christianity.'[1] John, unlike St Paul, does not speak of his own mystical experiences, but his doctrine is the ideal of Christian Mysticism, influenced by the writings of both Plato and the Jewish philosopher Philo (b. 20 BC). John teaches in his first Epistle that 'God is Love', 'God is Light', and 'God is Spirit', and he emphasizes, above all, the Incarnation, developing further the concept upheld by Philo of the 'Logos' – 'God revealed ... the Word and the Image of God, Who is man's chief helper in his striving towards the Divine.'[2] Consequently, St John views the Incarnation as an event which brought the Godhead, the pure Being, within the reach of intelligent devotion. 'No one has ever seen God; it is his only Son, who is close to the Father's heart, who has made him known.' (1:18) God sent His only Son to us that we might be saved – 'The Word became flesh, he lived among us, and we saw his glory.' (1:14)

The Incarnation emphasizes the bond between God and man, who is himself of Divine origin, but unless man is 'born from above' he cannot know God and receive eternal life. The Way of Purgation is the key to unlock the kingdom of God: 'Anyone who loves his life loses it; anyone who hates his life in this world will keep it for eternal life.' (12:24)

It was St Paul, originally a Jew and a Roman citizen named Saul, who carried the Gospel into the Hellenistic world. His own vision of God was that of Christ Incarnate on the road to Damascus. This was a deeply mystical experience which left him blind and unable to eat or drink for three days, after which he converted to Christianity and changed his name to Paul. It is recorded in Acts of the Apostles:

St Paul experienced a mystical vision of Christ which led to his conversion to Christianity.

'Saul, Saul, why are you persecuting me?' 'Who are you, Lord?' he asked, and the answer came, 'I am Jesus, whom you are persecuting. Get up and go into the city, and you will be told what you are to do.' (9:4-6)

Paul's understanding of the death and resurrection of Christ led to a firm belief in the law of redemption which served as the foundation of his teaching. His writings make plain his conviction that we all partake of the Divine nature, 'since it is in him that we live, and move, and exist'. (Acts 17:28) Through Christ, 'the victory over sin and death was won for us, but it must also be won in us.'[3] 'And you were dead, through the crimes and the sins which used to make up your way of life when you were living by the principles of this world', he writes to the Ephesians (2:1). The perfect man is that individual who has come 'to the measure of the stature of the fullness of Christ', (4:13) and he echoes the doctrine of the Mystic Way when he asserts: 'We should wash ourselves clean of everything that pollutes either body or spirit, bringing our sanctification to completion in the fear of God.' (Corinthians 7:1)

[1] W. R. Inge, Christian Mysticism, London 1933
[2] Margaret Smith, History of Mysticism, London 1930
[3] W. R. Inge, Christian Mysticism, London 1933

St Paul's teachings were based on his belief in the redemption of all men through the death and resurrection of Christ.

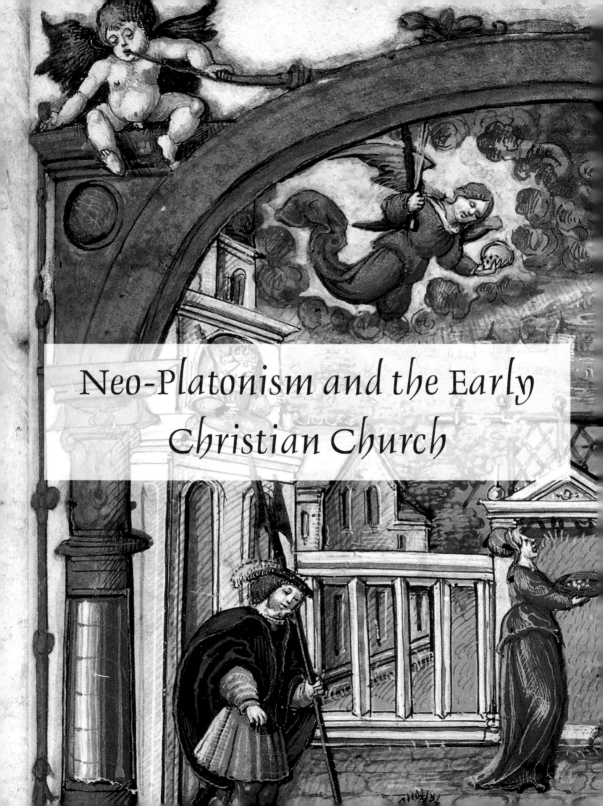

Neo-Platonism and the Early Christian Church

Neo-Platonism and the Early Christian Church

❧

> Beholding this Being—resting, rapt, in the vision and possession of so lofty a loveliness, growing to Its likeness—what beauty can the soul yet lack? For This, the Beauty supreme, the absolute and the primal, fashions Its lovers to Beauty and makes them also worthy of love.
>
> Plotinus (203—262 AD), *The Ennead*

IN THE THIRD CENTURY of the Christian era, the spiritual philosophies of Plato were revived and elaborated upon by many philosophers and scholars including Plotinus, Porphyry, Proclus and Origen, whose system of thought, which became known as Neo-Platonism, exerted a far-reaching influence on Christian theology lasting right up until the eighteenth century. Plotinus, himself a non-Christian, is considered the chief exponent of Neo-Platonism, since it was his theory of the Chain of Being which left the deepest impression on Christian Mysticism.

Later philosophers expanded on the spiritual theories of Plato and produced a new system of thought known as Neo-Platonism.

Plotinus

Plotinus pronounced that the universe was a vast chain in which every being formed a link. At the head of this chain is the Primeval Being, the Universal Good, the Perfect Beauty, who is above existence. From this Universal Good there emanates the Universal Intelligence or Mind, of whom all other minds partake, which occupies the world of Ideas and self-conscious reason, i.e., 'the ultimate form in which things are regarded by Intelligence, or by God'.[1] Completing this Trinity of the Godhead is the Universal soul, broken down into individual souls which occupy the sphere of imperfect reality, the phenomenal world.

'The souls of men are not disconnected from their origin', declared Plotinus. Everything flows from the Universal Good and everything desires to flow back towards it, but only those who 'cut away everything' that is not the One can hope to experience God. The nature of the world-soul is triple, and from this trifold nature is derived the three target stages of perfection along the Mystic Way, or as Plotinus described it, 'the flight of the alone to the Alone.' To attain the vision of God:

'is for those that will follow the upward path, who will divest themselves of all that we have put on in our descent – until passing, on the upward way, all this is other than God, each in the solitude of himself shall behold that solitary-dwelling Existence, the Apart, the Unmingled, the Pure, that from Which all things depend, for which all look and live and act and know, the Source of Life and of Intellection and of Being.'[2]

Mysticism and the Early Christian Church

One of the most important mystics of the early Christian Church was St Augustine. Born in the fourth century in what is now Algeria, North Africa, he was the first to properly introduce the ideas of Plotinus and the Neo-Platonists

The man in search of the vision of God will find it only through solitary contemplation.

into the Christianity of the Latin West, combining a penetrating intellectual vision with a passionate, all-encompassing love of God. For many years a follower of Manichaeism, adhering to a belief in the dualistic powers of light and darkness, Augustine was captivated by the mystical speculations of Plotinus which led him towards the Christian faith. Echoing Plotinus and Plato, he speaks frequently of the 'Beauty of God' and of the soul's quest for a return to God. He acknowledges that the way to God is from 'without to within, and from within to something that surpasses even the highest summit of the soul.'[3] This journey can only take place in stages – first purgation, then illumination, culminating in the ecstasy of union so frequently mentioned in his *Confessions*:

What is this which shines on me and pierces my heart without hurting it? I shudder and am aflame at the same time: I shudder, because I am so dissimilar to it, and I am aflame, because I am so similar to it. It is Wisdom, Wisdom itself which shines on me, breaking up my cloudiness, which yet covers me once more as I fall away from it through the darkness and rubble of my troubles.

(*Confessions*, 11.9)

St Augustine was one of the most important mystics of the early Christian Church.

> *Unto this Darkness which is beyond Light we pray that we may come, and through loss of sight and knowledge may see and know That Which transcends sight and knowledge, by the very fact of not seeing and knowing; for this is real sight and knowledge.*
>
> *Dionysius (c. 500 AD), Mystical Theology*

Dionysius the Areopagite

The true identity of Dionysius is uncertain, but it is thought that he was a Syrian monk and a disciple of St Paul who lived at the end of the fifth century AD. 'Pseudo-Dionysius' is the literary term now given to the unknown writers of the mystical treatises associated with Dionysius. One of the most important of these writings was a short treatise called The Mystical Theology, a fusion of Neo-Platonism and Oriental speculation which had a profound influence on much of Christian Mysticism of the Middle Ages, especially the German Mysticism of Meister Eckhart. For the first time in mystical literature, the notion of God as the 'Divine Dark' was introduced. St John had described God as the Divine Light, but in opposition to this, The Mystical Theology stressed the 'negative way' (via negativa) – the importance of 'divine ignorance' and 'unknowing' as the soul's route to the highest truth.

Statue of St Paul. His teachings encouraged many disciples, who expanded the philosophies of mystical theology.

'The mystic must leave behind all things, both in the sensible and the intelligible worlds' wrote Pseudo-Dionysius, 'till he enters into the darkness or knowing nothing that is truly mystical... Our highest knowledge of God consists in mystic ignorance.' This system of mysticism, closely aligned to all Oriental Mysticism and the Buddhist concept of Nirvāna, became widely popular in Europe from the ninth century onwards as a result of the translation from Greek to Latin by the Irish theologian, John Scotus Erigena.

The Desert Fathers

During the first three centuries of the Christian era, before Christianity became the official religion of the Empire, martyrdom was a crucial expression of the soul's perfection. During the fourth century, however, when the persecution of Christians ceased and the Christian religion lost some of its heroic fervour, a number of followers began seeking an alternative way. Turning their backs on the world, they established themselves in the deserts of Egypt and Syria with the intention of leading lives of contemplation, deprivation and physical mortification.

A Bishop Martyr — Martyrdom was the greatest expression of the soul's perfection and devotion.

The most important of these 'Desert Fathers' as they came to be known, was St Antony, who is now hailed as the founder of Christian monastic life. Born into a wealthy Egyptian family, Antony chose to live a life of rigorous asceticism, moving to the corner of a remote, solitary Roman fort in the desert. Throughout his long life, Antony attracted many pilgrims and admirers. Before his death at the age of one hundred, he instructed his most trusted disciple, Saint Pachomius, to found the first monasteries devoted to prayer and communal work.

[1]   W. R. Inge, *Christian Mysticism*, London 1933
[2]   Plotinus, *The Enneads*, trans. S. McKenna, London 1956
[3]   Hilda Graef, *The Light and the Rainbow*, London 1959

St Antony, the first Christian monk, left his life of comfort to live in deprivation and solitude.

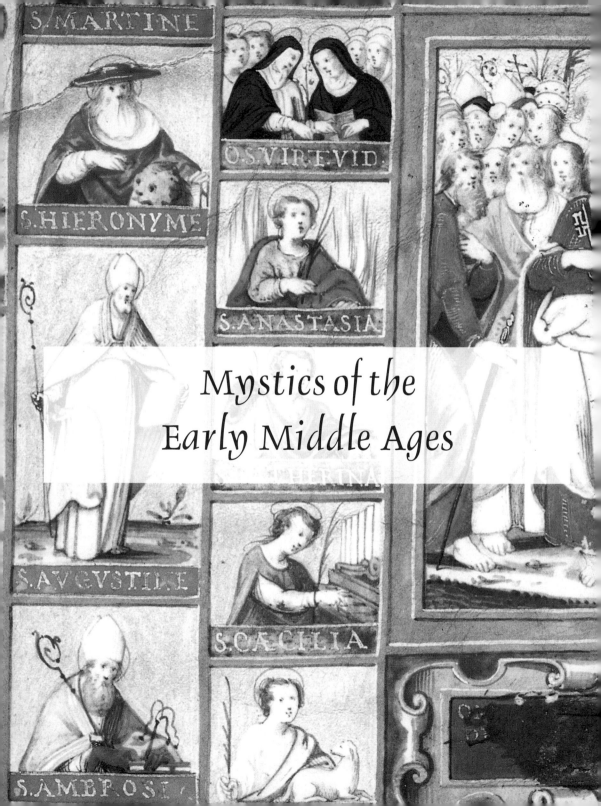

Mystics of the
Early Middle Ages

OSINNOCENT

S·ANTONI

S·STEPHANE

S·BERNARDE

S·DOMINICE

S·LAVRENTI

S·FRANCISCE

S·VINCENTI

Mystics of the
Early Middle Ages

❁

For it is the way of the perfect lover not only to love
what he loves more than himself, but also in some sort to
hate himself for the sake of what he loves. So you are to
do with yourself. You must loathe and tire of all that
goes on in your mind and your will unless it is God.

Anonymous, *The Cloud of Unknowing* – 14th Century

BY THE TIME OF ST AUGUSTINE'S DEATH in the early fifth century, the ancient classical civilization of the Greeks and the Romans was already only a shadow of its former glorious self. Wave after wave of northern barbarians descended upon the Roman world, dragging Europe into that dismal era known as the Dark Ages. It was during this period, however, that monasticism was given its greatest lease of life, as more and more individuals, appalled by the violence of the invasions, withdrew from the world in order to take up an ascetic life in a

The appeal of monastic life for both men and women increased as war and chaos invaded Europe.

Christian community devoted to prayer and penitential practices. These men and women became known as the Devotional Mystics.

The Devotional Mystics

St Bernard of Clairvaux (1090-1153) is one of the most outstanding of the Devotional Mystics, born at that period when Europe had begun to emerge from the Dark Ages heading towards a century of growth and renewal. This was the age of the great Crusades, of the birth of Chivalry, of the preoccupation in society with the meaning of pure and ardent love. At the age of twenty-two, Bernard abandoned his home to enter the small monastery at Citeaux, France. Three years later he became Abbot of Clairvaux and for the next thirty-eight years lived a life of intense activity, governing his own monastery, advising Popes and princes, as well as writing a number of highly influential treatises and travelling all over Europe to deliver his instructive teachings on Christianity.

It was Bernard who promoted the detailed consideration of Christ's human life and its application to the moral and spiritual needs of Christians. The idea, in itself, was not new, but up until the Middle Ages, emphasis had been placed on the Divine majesty of Christ, rather than on his poignant humanity. In his *Sermons on the Canticle*, St Bernard sums up the importance to spiritual life of an appreciation of the Incarnate Christ's humanity:

... When man prays there is present with him the sacred image of the God-man ... and whatever else such meditation may present, if necessary, it either urges the soul to the love of the virtues, or expels the vices of the flesh ... This, I believe, is the principal cause why the invisible God would be seen in the flesh and converse with men, that he might first draw all the affections of those carnal men who could as yet love only carnally to the salutary love of his flesh and thus gradually lead them on to spiritual love. (20:6)

St Bernard of Clairvaux, depicted here with St Francis of Assisi, was a prominent figure of the Devotional Mystics. He travelled across Europe, spreading the Christian word.

Bernard was deeply concerned with the problem of loving his God. He developed further the imagery of the Spiritual Marriage between God and his follower and adopted the Mystic Way as 'a continuous apprenticeship in love'. As F. C. Happold puts it, 'The fact of earthly love is St Bernard's starting-point. There is first the love of oneself and one's own interests; then love in a higher form, the love of one's neighbour; and then love at its highest, the love of God; and in this there is a reciprocal action which has its fount in God.'[1]

Another well-known Devotional Mystic was St Francis of Assisi (1182-1226) who developed further the concept of the humanity of Christ through the evocation of His suffering, bringing to the very centre of Christianity the image of the crucified Saviour. St Francis, founder of the Franciscan Order, devoted his entire life to becoming more and more like Christ, not only through his preaching, but through the physical, day-to day imitation of Christ's poverty, isolation and suffering. Obedience, poverty and chastity were the three solemn vows of all monastic orders. Prayer was emphasized as the means by which the inward feelings might be cleansed leading to mystic union with the one true and highest God. The crowning mystical glory of St Francis' life of humility and contemplation came two years before his death on Mount Alverna when he experienced the ultimate gratification of mystical faith – a vision of the crucified Christ which resulted in the appearance of identical wounds or 'stigmata' on his own body.

The Book of the Lover and the Beloved

One other Medieval Mystic associated with the Franciscans deserves a brief mention here. Ramon Lull, a lay member of the Order, born in Catalan in the thirteenth century, was responsible for the authorship of *The Book of the Lover and the Beloved*. Divided into three hundred and sixty six verses, one for each day of

*Opposite: The teachings of St Bernard emphasized the humanity of Christ rather than His Divine majesty.
Overleaf: St Francis of Assisi devoted his life to achieving the Union through imitation of Christ's poverty, isolation and suffering.*

the year, it is a volume which sets out to interpret the Mystic Life in layman's terms, with the intention that 'the hearts of men might be moved to true contrition, their eyes to abundance of tears, and their wills and understandings to loftier flights in the contemplation of God.' [2]

'What meanest thou by love?' said the Beloved. And the Lover answered: 'It is to bear on one's heart the sacred marks and the sweet words of the Beloved. It is to long for Him with desire and with tears. It is boldness. It is fervour. It is fear. It is the desire for the Beloved above all things. It is that which causes the Lover to grow faint when he hears the Beloved's praises. It is that in which I die daily, and in which is all my will.'

(Verse 165)

[1]   F. C. Happold, *Mysticism*, London 1970
[2]   Ramon Lull, *The Book of the Lover and the Beloved*, trans. E. Allison Peers, London 1923

Many Medieval books and manuscripts were produced expounding the theories of Mysticism.

Mysticism in the
Late Middle Ages

Mysticism in the
Late Middle Ages

�֎

> God is not seen except by blindness, nor known
> except by ignorance, nor understood except by fools.
> According to St Augustine, no soul can get to God
> who goes not without creature and seeks not God
> without likeness. And that is the meaning of Christ's
> words, 'Cast out first the beam out of thine own eye
> and then wash the mote out of another's eye.'
>
> Meister Eckhart (1260—1327), Sermons and Collations, LXXVI

AT THE SAME TIME AS CHRISTIAN MYSTICISM developed towards an appreciation of the humanity of Christ, the Dionysian tradition of the 'via negativa', the Darkness and formlessness of the Divine Being, continued to dominate the thinking of certain German and continental Mystics, the most prominent and influential of whom was Meister Eckhart.

Opposite and overleaf: Meister Eckhart believed in the distinction between 'God', in the form of the Holy Trinity, and the 'Godhead' from which the power of God flows.

> It hath been said, that there is of nothing so much in
> hell as of self-will. The which is true, for there is
> nothing else there than self-will, and if there were no
> self-will there would be no Devil and no hell.
>
> *Theologica Germanica,* Ch. XLIX

Meister Eckhart and the German Mystics

One of the most controversial figures of Medieval mysticism, Meister
Eckhart (1260-1327) made clear the distinction between the 'Godhead' – that
unknown Being above all nature who cannot be the object of worship and 'God' –
the divine power at work within the universe comprising of the Father, Son and
Holy Ghost, the Trinity which flows from the Godhead and is inherent in the
Godhead itself. A member of the Dominican Order, he preached that when the
soul has been purified, she pours herself out into the 'supernatural of the pure
Godhead' and she is one with God and He with her. According to Eckhart's
teaching, 'beneath sense perception, beneath the sensuous will, beneath the higher powers of memory, reason, and reasonable will, lies the soul, the apex, the
spark, the heaven within. It is here that man may find God.' [1] Yet in order to
attain this goal, the soul must perform the ultimate sacrifice, the 'most ultimate
death' and even lose contact with God, in order to become truly divine.

Opposite: *Eckhart preached that at the purification
of the soul, it combines with the pure Godhead and thus becomes one with God.*
Overleaf: *St Teresa of Avila, depicted here with the Holy Family, was a well known female Christian mystic.*

Eckhart renounced all external influences and opposed the notion that a truly religious life could only be properly fulfilled if the individual removed himself from the world. 'You need not go into the desert and fast,' he declared, 'a crowd is often more lonely than a wilderness, and small things harder to do than great.' For Eckhart, the mystic union each man aspires to is already within the soul of man:

'There is in the soul something which is above the soul, Divine, simple, a pure nothing; rather nameless than named, rather unknown than known ... Sometimes I have called it a power, sometimes an uncreated light, and sometimes a Divine spark ... It is absolute and free from all names and all forms, just as God is free and absolute in Himself.'

But by asserting that 'the eye in which I see God is the same as that with which He sees me', or that 'God begets His Son in me', Eckhart laid himself open to charges of pantheism, or self-deification. He was not alone among the Mystics accused of heresy. His successors Suso and Tauler, together with other well-known Mystics, including Amuary of Bene, St John of the Cross, Miguel Molinos, and François Fénelon were also victims of the religious purges which began in Europe immediately after Eckhart's death and lasted well into the late Middle Ages.

Women Mystics

It would be negligent to conclude this short study of Christian Mysticism without drawing some measure of attention to the female Mystics notable for their contribution to the movement over the centuries. The list is a very long one, however, and includes such well-known personages as Hildegard of Bingen, Elisabeth of Schoenau, Angela of Foligno, Catherine of Siena, Teresa of Avila, Madame Guyon, Madame Acarie and Julian of Norwich.

Many women have contributed to the movement of Mysticism over the centuries.

> And when I looked, I beheld God who spake with me.
> But if thou seekest to know that which I beheld, I can
> tell thee nothing, save that I beheld a fulness and a
> clearness, and felt them within me so abundantly that I
> can in no wise describe it, nor give any likeness thereof.
>
> Angela of Foligno (c. 1470—1540), The Book of Divine Consolation

Julian of Norwich (1343-after 1413), who represents a distinctively English tradition of European Mysticism, deserves particular mention here, for it has not been possible in a volume of this size to discuss any of the other Mystics of Medieval England, among them Richard Rolle, Margerie Kempe and Walter Hilton. Julian, whose mystical views are firmly founded on the teachings of Plato, experienced a series of powerful visions during an illness in her early thirties which she recorded twenty years later in her Sixteen Revelations of Divine Love. These memoirs recall how in each vision she perceived the three properties of God: Life, Love and Light. Echoing a fundamental belief of all Mystics, she maintains that the soul is of one nature with God. Through the power of prayer the human will can be restored to the Divine Will and attain a likeness to God:

Opposite: *After a series of mystical visions, Julian of Norwich came to believe that the power of prayer could lead to union with God.*
Overleaf: *Christian miracles and mystical visions played an important part in the teachings of Mysticism.*

'Beseeching is a true, gracious, lasting will of the soul, oned and fastened into the will of our Lord – our Lord willeth to have our prayer, because with His grace He maketh us like to Himself in condition as we are in kind.'

During the Middle Ages the Church attempted and failed to eradicate the Mystic's individual vision of his soul's quest for union with God, although it did succeed in undermining that vision through a policy of systematic persecution. Mysticism survived, none the less, and in post-Reformation England it was given a new lease of life through the Cambridge Platonists who drew inspiration from both Plato and Plotinus.

The individual's quest for communion with the Divine is as timeless as it is universal. The essence of Mysticism, in the words of E. Underhill, 'is simply to participate here and now in real and eternal life, in the fullest, deepest sense which is possible to man. It is to share as a free and conscious agent in the joyous travail of the universe, its mighty, onward sweep through pain and glory to its home in God.'[2]

[1] F. C. Happold, *Mysticism*, London 1970
[2] E. Underhill, *Mysticism*, London 1912

Opposite: *The purity of the Christ child and his union with God, personifies the goal sought by Christian Mystics.*
Overleaf: *Through the power of prayer the human will can be restored to the Divine Will and attain a likeness to God.*

Suggested Further Reading

※

Butler, Dom Cuthbert, *Western Mysticism*, London 1927

Happold, F .C., *Mysticism*, London 1990

Inge, W. R., *Christian Mysticism*, London 1933

Julian of Norwich, *Revelations of Divine Love*, London 1901

Lull, Ramon, *The Book of the Lover and the Beloved*, trans. E. Allison Peers, London 1923

Meister Eckhart, trans. J Evans, London 1924

More, Paul Elmer, *Christian Mysticism*, London 1932

Plotinus, *The Enneads*, trans. S. McKenna, London 1956

Smith, Margaret, *History of Mysticism*, London 1930

Underhill, E, *Mysticism*, London 1912

Wolters, Clifton, trans. *The Cloud of Unknowing*, London 1961

Illustration Notes

❋

Page 9 *A Bishop Martyr — Wing of an Altarpiece* by the Danube School. Courtesy of Christie's Images. **Page 10** *Madonna and Child Enthroned* attributed to Bernardino Zenale da Treviglio. Courtesy of Christie's Images. **Pages 12-13** Detail from *The Lamentation* by Antonio Vasquez. Courtesy of Christie's Images. **Page 15** *An Angel Protecting a Soul in the Balance from the Devil* by Guariento di Arpo. Courtesy of Christie's Images. **Page 16** *A Monk in His Study* by Leandro Bassano. Courtesy of Christie's Images. **Page 19** *Madonna and Child Enthroned* attributed to Bernardino Zenale da Treviglio. Courtesy of Christie's Images. **Pages 20-1** *The Lamentation* by Antonio Vasquez. Courtesy of Christie's Images. **Page 22** *Book of Prayers: Road to Calvary.* Courtesy of Christie's Images. **Page 25** *A Hermit Saint at Prayer* by a Follower of Gerrit Dou. Courtesy of Christie's Images. **Page 27** *Book of Hours: God* by a Master of Morgan. Courtesy of Visual Arts Library. **Page 29** detail from *Book of Hours: King David with His Harp.* Courtesy of Christie's Images. **Pages 30-1** Detail from *The Lamentation* by Antonio Vasquez. Courtesy of Christie's Images. **Page 33** *The Death of Socrates* by Salvator Rosa. Courtesy of Christie's Images. **Page 34** *The Temptation* by Jacob Jordaens. Courtesy of Christie's Images. **Page 37** *Book of Hours: King David with His Harp.* Courtesy of Christie's Images. **Pages 38-9** *Book of Hours: St John on Patmos* by Jean Poyet. Courtesy of Christie's Images. **Page 40** *Saint Paul Preaching: Initial "P" from an Illuminated Choirbook.* Courtesy of Christie's Images. **Page 43** *The Crucifixion with Two Prophets* by Juan de Levi. Courtesy of Christie's Images. **Pages 44-5** Detail from *Book of Hours: King David with His Harp.* Courtesy of Christie's Images. **Page 47** *Bearded Philosopher, His Head Resting on His Hand* by Ubaldo Gandolfi. Courtesy of Christie's Images. **Page 49** *Saint Benedict* by Andrea di Bartolo. Courtesy of Christie's Images. **Page 50** *All Saints Including St Augustine.* Courtesy of Christie's Images. **Page 53** *Spanish Polychrome and Giltwood Figure of St Paul.* Courtesy of Christie's Images. **Page 55** *A Bishop Martyr — Wing of an Altarpiece* by the Danube School. Courtesy of Christie's Images. **Page 56** *Saint Anthony of Padua* by Francesco de Mura. Courtesy of Christie's Images. **Pages 58-9** Detail from *All Saints Including St Augustine.* Courtesy of Christie's Images. **Page 60** *Saint Ottilie* by the Circle of Jan Polak. Courtesy of Christie's Images. **Page 63** *St Francis of Assisi and St Bernard of Clairvaux* by the Circle of Gerard David. Courtesy of Christie's Images. **Page 65** *Icon: Christ.* Courtesy of Visual Arts Library. **Pages 66-7** *Saint Francis Receiving the Stigmata* by Francesco Raibolini. Courtesy of Christie's Images. **Page 69** *Christ Enthroned and Evangelists* by a Master of Morgan. Courtesy of Visual Arts Library. **Pages 70-1** Detail from *The Crucifixion with Two Prophets* by Juan de Levi. Courtesy of Christie's Images. **Page 73** *The Holy Trinity with Mary and St Sebastian* (Museum der Bildenden Künste, Leipzig). Courtesy of Visual Arts Library. **Pages 74-5** Detail from *The Holy Trinity with Mary and St Sebastian* (Museum der Bildenden Künste, Leipzig). Courtesy of Visual Arts Library. **Page 77** *A Priest Administering the Host to a Dominican Nun at a Squint* by the Ferrarese School. Courtesy of Christie's Images. **Pages 78-9** *The Holy Family with Saint Teresa of Avila* by Elisabetta Sirani. Courtesy of Christie's Images. **Page 80** *Six Female Saints* by Carlo da Camerino. Courtesy of Christie's Images. **Page 83** *Book of Hours: The Virgin.* Courtesy of Christie's Images. **Pages 84-5** *Pentecost: Large Historiated Initial "S".* Courtesy of Christie's Images. **Page 86** Detail from *The Holy Family with Saint Teresa of Avila* by Elisabetta Sirani. Courtesy of Christie's Images. **Pages 88-9** Detail from *Six Female Saints* by Carlo da Camerino. Courtesy of Christie's Images.

Index

❋

Index

❀